SALAJ SHEKHAR

Democracy of Plato

An Examination of Democracy Through Plato's Lens

First edition

Contents

Acknowledgments

I would like to express my sincere gratitude to everyone who supported and guided me throughout the journey of writing this book. My heartfelt thanks to my teacher, **Kavita Ma'am**, and my friend, **Fazal**, who took the time to read the manuscript and provide valuable feedback and encouragement. Their insights and suggestions helped improve the clarity and quality of this work. I would also like to give a special thanks to my classmate **Samridhi**, who designed the cover page of this book. Her creativity, patience, and effort played an important role in giving the book its visual identity. Lastly, I am grateful to all those who indirectly supported and motivated me during this journey. This book would not have been possible without your encouragement and belief.

Prologue

Democracy is often treated as an answer rather than a question. It is inherited, praised, and defended long before it is examined. For many of us, it becomes familiar before it becomes understood.

This book does not begin with *rejection or praise*. It begins with *doubt*. Not the kind that seeks destruction, but the kind that seeks clarity. The kind that asks whether what we believe is true because it has been tested, or simply because it has been repeated.

Plato lived in a world where democracy was new, powerful, and deeply trusted. He watched it work, fail, and reshape the minds of those who lived under it. His critique was not an attack on freedom, but a challenge to complacency. He asked questions most societies prefer to avoid.

The pages that follow do not attempt to defend Plato or condemn democracy. They attempt something quieter. They look at democracy through Plato's lens and ask what kind of thinking it encourages, what kind of people it shapes, and what kind of power it creates.

This is not a book of answers.
It is a book of questions.

1

Plato and the Rule of the Many

Democracy is usually defined as a system of government in which power belongs to the people, either directly or through elected representatives.

From childhood, we are told that democracy is the best form of government. It is taught as the fairest system, the most just, and the most reasonable way to organize a society. And honestly, it does make sense. Giving people a voice feels right. Letting everyone participate feels fair. Democracy appears to be the natural opposite of tyranny.

But is it really that simple?

Around 428–423 BC, a Greek philosopher was born who did exactly that.

Plato, now considered one of the foundational thinkers of Western philosophy, is also remembered as one of the earliest critics of democracy. His criticism was not driven by anger or ideology. It came from a concern about how decisions are made and who should make them.

Plato believed democracy was dangerous. That claim sounds extreme today, but his reasoning was practical. He questioned whether it made sense for an entire population to choose its leaders when most people lacked knowledge of governance. Is a system truly rational, he asked, if it treats all opinions as equally valuable even when they are not equally informed?

> To explain his concern, Plato used a simple thought experiment. *Imagine you are on a ship caught in a violent storm. The ship must be guided carefully or it will sink. You are given two choices. One option is to allow a trained sailor, someone who has studied navigation and understands the sea, to take control. The other is to hold a vote among the passengers and let them decide who should steer the ship.*

Most people would not hesitate. You would choose the sailor. Not because the passengers are bad people, but because sailing a ship requires knowledge. Letting popularity decide in that moment would be reckless. Plato believed governing a state was no different.

In *The Republic*, Socrates compares the population to a strong but near-sighted ship's master. The sailors, representing politicians and demagogues, fight among themselves for control. They flatter the master, promise rewards, and claim knowledge they do not actually possess. The true navigator, the philosopher, is ignored and dismissed as useless, even though he alone understands how to guide the ship safely.

The problem, Plato argued, is not participation itself. The problem is that democracy rewards persuasion more than understanding. Those who speak well gain power, not necessarily those who think well. Opinion rises through numbers rather than truth. Over time, confidence replaces competence and popularity replaces wisdom.

This does not mean democracy has no value. Plato understood why people were drawn to it. Equality matters. Freedom matters. Having a voice matters. What troubled him was the assumption that these values automatically lead to good decisions. Democracy, he believed, focuses more on the right to choose than on the ability to choose wisely.

His question still feels uncomfortable.

If we would never let passengers vote on how to sail a ship, why do we let citizens vote on how to run a nation?

Is governance simple enough that expertise does not matter, or have we confused fairness with correctness?

This chapter does not attempt to answer that question. It only asks it. Before democracy can be defended or rejected, it must be examined honestly. Through Plato's lens, democracy becomes not just a political system, but a way of thinking, one that deserves closer attention than it usually receives.

2

Plato on Opinion and Power

Democracy gives power to opinion. That fact is often overlooked because opinion feels harmless. Everyone has one, and everyone feels entitled to express it. In a democratic system, opinion does not remain private or personal. It enters the public sphere, where it begins to shape laws, leaders, and collective decisions.

Plato was deeply concerned by this. His concern was not that people held opinions, but that opinions were treated as if they were knowledge. In a democracy, an idea does not gain authority because it is true or well understood. It gains authority because it is shared by many. Numbers, not understanding, become the source of power.

Plato made a careful distinction between knowledge and opinion. Knowledge, in his view, requires training, discipline, and a willingness to accept uncertainty. It grows slowly and demands effort. Opinion forms quickly. It often feels complete even when it is shallow. Most importantly, opinion does not recognize its own limits. It speaks with confidence even when it lacks understanding.

* * *

Equality and Plato

Democracy, Plato believed, erases this distinction in practice. When every opinion is given equal political weight, knowledge loses its special role. The person who has spent years studying an issue stands on the same ground as the person who has only encountered it briefly. Both are heard. Both are counted. Both influence outcomes.

This equality disturbed him, not because he despised ordinary people, but because he understood how persuasion works. In a system where power depends on approval, those who communicate simply and confidently gain influence. Those who speak cautiously, who acknowledge complexity, or who admit uncertainty are easily ignored. Democracy, he believed, rewards persuasion more than understanding.

He observed that opinion is especially vulnerable to emotion. Fear, anger, hope, and pride shape belief far more easily than careful reasoning. In democratic societies, emotional appeal becomes a political tool. Leaders learn to excite rather than educate, to reassure rather than challenge. Truth becomes less important than resonance.

Over time, this creates a dangerous habit. Ideas are judged not by whether they are accurate, but by whether they are popular. Complex truths are avoided because they demand patience. Simple answers dominate because they are easy to repeat. In such an environment, opinion does not merely participate in power. It replaces judgment.

Plato feared that democracy encourages a false confidence. Those who understand least often speak with the greatest certainty, while those who understand most hesitate. The knowledgeable recognize complexity and doubt themselves. The ignorant see no such difficulty. When opinion governs, confidence is mistaken for competence.

This does not mean Plato believed people were incapable of learning. His concern was structural. Democracy, as a system, does not require understanding from those who participate in it. Everyone may vote, but no one is required to know. Opinion fills the space where education should be.

For Plato, the greatest danger was not disagreement, but the absence of standards. In a world ruled by opinion, there is no clear way to distinguish wisdom from noise. Truth competes with falsehood on equal terms. The louder voice often wins.

Plato did not argue that opinion should be silenced. That would contradict the very freedom democracy values. Instead, he questioned whether a system built on opinion could ever consistently produce wise decisions without cultivating knowledge. Democracy offers freedom of expression, but it does not guarantee understanding.

If Chapter 1 questioned who should rule, this chapter asks a quieter question: what kind of thinking does a ruling system encourage? For Plato, democracy encouraged opinion to rise faster than knowledge. Whether that tension can ever be resolved remains uncertain.

This tension matters because it shapes not only political outcomes but the habits of thought within a society. When opinion is rewarded more quickly than understanding, people learn to speak before they learn to think. Confidence becomes a substitute for clarity, and repetition replaces reflection. Over time, this changes what a society values. Depth begins to feel unnecessary, patience feels unproductive, and careful thought appears weak.

Plato feared that such a culture would drift away from wisdom without realizing it. Not through force or deception, but through comfort. When opinion rules easily, thinking deeply becomes optional. Whether democracy can preserve freedom while still demanding understanding is a question Plato leaves open, and one that remains unresolved.

3

Plato's Crowd

Plato did not think of people only as individuals. He paid close attention to what happens when individuals become a crowd. Alone, a person may hesitate, reflect, and doubt their own judgment. In a group, that same person often changes. Responsibility spreads out. Emotion intensifies. Judgment weakens.

This transformation deeply concerned him. For him, the danger of democracy was not only that opinion gained power, but that opinion behaved differently once it became collective. In a crowd, beliefs are reinforced rather than examined. Agreement feels safe. Doubt feels uncomfortable. What begins as uncertainty slowly hardens into certainty, not because it has been tested, but because it has been shared.

Plato observed that crowds do not think patiently. They move quickly toward conclusions. They prefer simple answers to difficult questions and clear targets to complex problems. In such an environment, careful reasoning appears slow and ineffective. Those who pause to think are seen as weak. Those who speak boldly, even without depth, appear confident and strong.

This is where manipulation becomes possible.

Plato understood that a crowd does not need to be convinced through truth. It only needs to be moved through emotion. Fear, anger, pride, and hope spread easily among large groups. Once emotion takes hold, reasoning retreats. A skilled speaker can guide belief not by explaining reality, but by shaping how the crowd feels about it.

In democratic societies, this allows persuasion to replace understanding. Leaders are chosen not for their insight, but for their ability to excite, reassure, or provoke. Complex explanations are avoided because they demand effort. Emotional narratives dominate because they demand nothing. The crowd responds to tone more than content.

Plato believed this dynamic rewarded performance over truth. Those who tell people what they want to hear rise quickly. Those who challenge beliefs or introduce discomfort are pushed aside. The crowd does not reject wisdom intentionally. It simply prefers comfort.

Athens and the Power of the Jury

Plato's fears were not abstract. He watched them unfold in his own city. Athens, often celebrated as the birthplace of democracy, placed immense trust in the judgment of the many. Its courts were run by large juries made up of ordinary citizens, sometimes numbering in the hundreds. These jurors were not trained in law or philosophy. They were expected to listen, feel, and decide.

One event shaped Plato more than any other. *His teacher, Socrates, was put on trial by an Athenian jury. He was accused of corrupting the youth and disrespecting the gods of the city. The charges were vague, emotional, and deeply tied to public sentiment rather than clear evidence.*

Socrates refused to flatter the jury. He did not beg for sympathy or appeal to fear. He spoke calmly, questioned assumptions, and challenged his accusers. In doing so, he violated an unspoken rule of democratic judgment. He refused to please the crowd. The result was fatal. The jury condemned him to death.

For Plato, this was not a tragic exception. It was a warning. Socrates was not executed by a tyrant or a king. He was executed by the people. The same system that claimed to value free thought silenced one of its most honest thinkers.

The jury did not act out of cruelty. It acted out of persuasion. Fear, resentment, and wounded pride guided its decision more than reason. The crowd believed it was acting justly. That belief made the outcome even more dangerous. When a society trusts collective judgment without standards, mistakes become righteousness, and injustice becomes law.

Athens showed Plato that democracy does not protect truth by default. It protects opinion. And opinion, when amplified by numbers, can destroy the very voices that challenge it.

Plato also noticed another danger within crowds: anonymity. When individuals act as part of a group, personal responsibility fades. Actions that would feel wrong alone become acceptable when shared. Responsibility dissolves into collective approval. This makes manipulation easier and accountability weaker. No one feels fully responsible for what the crowd believes or does.

This instability troubled Plato deeply. A crowd can be generous one moment and cruel the next. It can praise today and condemn tomorrow. What matters is not consistency, but mood. When power rests in such a force, leadership becomes an act of emotional management rather than rational direction.

Plato believed this was why philosophy struggles in democratic societies. Philosophy asks people to slow down, question themselves, and accept uncertainty. The crowd resists this. It prefers affirmation over challenge. The philosopher, who refuses to flatter, becomes isolated. He speaks truths the crowd does not want to hear.

Plato's concern reached beyond politics. When crowd thinking dominates, it shapes education, culture, and values. Young minds learn to repeat rather than reflect. Original thought feels risky. Conformity feels safe. Over time, the crowd becomes not just a political force, but a mental environment.

For Plato, the greatest danger was not that the crowd ruled, but that the crowd replaced thinking. When collective opinion becomes the highest authority, wisdom has nowhere to stand. Truth survives only when it agrees with the many.

This chapter does not claim that crowds are always wrong. It asks a more careful question. If democracy depends on collective judgment, how does it protect itself from the weaknesses of collective thinking? Plato saw this as one of democracy's deepest challenges, one that remains unresolved.

4

Plato in the Age of Voices

If Plato feared the crowd in ancient Athens, he would find the modern world difficult to ignore. Today, voices are everywhere. Opinion no longer waits for public gatherings or shared spaces. It appears instantly, spreads rapidly, and competes constantly for attention. What once required presence now requires only expression.

At first glance, this seems like the fulfillment of democracy's promise. More voices suggest more participation. More expression suggests greater freedom. The modern world appears to have solved the problem Plato feared by allowing everyone to speak. Yet Plato would likely pause here, not in celebration, but in caution. The existence of many voices does not guarantee that many are heard.

In the modern age, opinion does not merely exist. It competes. And in this competition, not all voices begin from the same position.

Plato warned that persuasion thrives where judgment weakens.

In a world saturated with voices, persuasion becomes more powerful, not less. Ideas are no longer encountered slowly or examined carefully. They are met quickly, reacted to immediately, and replaced just as fast. Speed favors reaction over reflection. Certainty appears stronger than doubt. Visibility becomes mistaken for truth.

This environment reshapes how people think. When attention is scarce, ideas are forced to simplify themselves to survive. Complexity becomes a disadvantage. Careful explanation feels excessive. Confidence, even when unsupported, feels persuasive. Plato feared that opinion would rise faster than knowledge. In the modern age, this gap widens continuously.

Yet noise alone is not the central problem. The deeper issue is structure.

Although many voices exist, attention is unevenly distributed. Some opinions travel farther, faster, and more frequently than others. This is where *established authority* enters. Established authority does not silence voices openly. It overwhelms them. Through influence, resources, and repetition, certain perspectives dominate public space while others fade quietly into obscurity.

This creates an illusion of equality. Everyone may speak, but not everyone is heard. Choice appears free, yet the range of visible choices is shaped in advance. People believe they are choosing independently, while their attention is guided subtly and persistently. Plato warned that persuasion does not require force. It requires access.

In this sense, corruption does not always appear as dishonesty or illegal action. It appears to be an influence. It appears when power learns how to shape opinion without announcing itself.

Established authority does not command belief directly. It cultivates familiarity. Ideas are repeated until they feel natural, then reasonable, and finally unquestionable. Exposure replaces evaluation.

Plato would recognize this pattern immediately. He warned that when opinion governs, truth must compete on unequal terms. The better argument does not always prevail. The better-positioned one often does. Democracy, in principle, values equality. In practice, it struggles against the concentration of influence.

Ostracism and Democratic Judgment

Plato did not need to imagine how democratic judgment could fail. Athens provided an example through the practice of ostracism. Each year, citizens were allowed to vote for the exile of one individual they believed posed a threat to the city. No crime had to be proven. No trial was required. A name written often enough was sufficient.

Ostracism was defended as a democratic safeguard. It claimed to protect the city from dangerous influence. In practice, it revealed how easily collective judgment could be shaped. Fear, rumor, resentment, and persuasion played a greater role than evidence. A person could be removed not for wrongdoing, but for being disliked, distrusted, or politically inconvenient.

The process appeared fair because it involved participation. Everyone could vote. Yet Plato would have seen its deeper flaw. The crowd was not asked to judge truth or guilt, only to express suspicion. Opinion, amplified by number, became authority. Once enough citizens were persuaded, exile followed naturally.

What troubled Plato was not the punishment itself, but the ease with which it occurred. The crowd believed it was acting rationally. In reality, it was reacting collectively, guided by mood and influence rather than careful judgment. Ostracism showed how democracy could remove individuals without tyranny, using participation itself as justification.

For Plato, this was proof that freedom of choice does not guarantee wisdom of choice. When decision-making depends on popularity rather than understanding, justice becomes unstable. The crowd does not need to be cruel. It only needs to be convinced.

Plato's concerns extend naturally into the modern world. When voices are ignored rather than silenced, frustration grows beneath the surface. People speak, yet feel unheard. Participation continues, but trust weakens. Citizens remain active, yet feel ineffective. Plato understood that such conditions make manipulation easier, not harder.

Emotion fills the space where understanding should exist. Anger, fear, and resentment become powerful tools. These emotions do not arise without cause, but they are often redirected. Established authority, skilled in managing perception, learns how to channel dissatisfaction without addressing its source. The crowd reacts, not because it has reasoned carefully, but because it feels overlooked.

Plato feared that democracy could slowly train people to mistake expression for influence. Speaking feels like acting. Reacting feels like thinking. Participation becomes emotional rather than reflective. Over time, citizens grow accustomed to noise while losing patience for depth. The system continues to function, but wisdom retreats.

This environment poses a serious challenge for philosophy. Philosophy demands slowness in a fast world. It demands uncertainty in a culture that rewards confidence. It asks people to question themselves in a space that encourages immediate judgment. The philosopher does not disappear, but his voice struggles to compete with repetition and volume.

Plato would not argue that modern democracy is doomed. His concern was never certain. It was a tendency. Systems shape habits of thought. When a system rewards attention over understanding, influence over insight, and repetition over truth, it quietly reshapes how people reason.

This chapter does not argue that voices should be limited or controlled. It asks something quieter and more difficult. In a world overflowing with voices, how does a society decide which deserve attention? If democracy promises equality of voice, how does it respond when authority concentrates influence rather than power?

Plato's fear was not that people would speak too much. It was that thinking would be replaced by noise, and judgment by visibility. Whether modern democracy can preserve freedom while resisting manipulation by established authority remains uncertain.

5

Education and the Problem of Preparation

Democracy is built on an idea that appears simple and moral. Every citizen should have an equal right in the making of collective decisions. This equality is given by democracy, also its greatest strength.

Democracy does not merely invite people to participate; it trusts them with power. This power affects laws, leadership, and the direction of society itself, but here, Plato was concerned with whether we could give those citizens the authority of collective decision-making.

Yet, the system offers this authority without knowing the people of the state.

Plato's concern was never that people were unworthy of power. It was that power, without education, that became threatening. He argued that the power of decision-making must be given to those who are educated.

Power without Training

In most areas of life, we believe power should come after preparation. We would never let someone perform surgery without training. An engineer must study before building something others will use. We do this because mistakes in these areas can harm people. When responsibility is heavy, learning comes first.

Politics is different.

In a democracy, political power is given simply by being born into the system. A person does not need to understand economics to help decide economic policy. They do not need to know history to shape a country's memory. They do not need to study law to influence legal decisions.

Many people defend this as morally right. If we ask for training before giving political power, it sounds unfair. It sounds like only a few people would be allowed to rule. Equality, people say, means everyone must be included. This feeling is understandable. No one wants power locked away from ordinary people.

But Plato believed this argument avoids an important question. It protects the right to participate, but it does not ask whether people are ready for the power they are given.

For Plato, power was never harmless. It made whatever guided it stronger. When power was guided by understanding, it could create justice. When it was guided by ignorance, it could spread mistakes. Democracy, by giving power to everyone right away, assumes that people already know how to use it wisely.

But assuming something is not the same as learning it.

Plato believed judgment must be taught. It does not appear on its own. Education, to him, was not just learning facts. It was learning how to think carefully, when to slow down, and how to admit what you do not know. Without this training, freedom can turn into carelessness.

Democracy does not wait for this kind of growth. Decisions are made before people have time to develop good judgment. The system keeps moving even when understanding has not caught up.

Plato worried that democracy confuses having the right to act with knowing how to act well. When someone makes a mistake in their private life, the damage is small. When mistakes are made in politics, everyone feels the effects. The errors do not stay personal. They become shared by the whole society.

Civic Authority without Competence

There is a clear difference between a private opinion and civic authority. A private opinion usually affects only the person who holds it. Civic authority affects many people at once. Democracy turns personal beliefs into public outcomes. What someone thinks does not stay in their own head. It becomes part of the decisions that shape everyone's life.

In a democracy, citizens do more than share opinions. They choose their leaders. They help decide which laws exist (indirectly, as those leaders will make laws). They help decide which values are supported by the state. This power is real. Yet it is given to the common people who are not educated.

When Plato spoke about competence, he did not mean that only smart or morally superior people should rule. He meant simply that governing a society is not easy; it requires knowledge, and when this power is given to the uneducated, it can, at worst, cause the society to break. *Competence means being aware that these difficulties exist.*

Democracy does not ask whether citizens understand this

complexity. It assumes that group decision-making will fix individual mistakes, as in a democracy, the large crowd will make a good decision. If one person lacks understanding, another person might correct them. Over time, the group is expected to reach good decisions.

Plato did not trust this idea. He did not believe that ignorance disappears when shared by many people. He believed it grows stronger. When many people share the same misunderstanding, it feels more convincing. An agreement creates confidence, not truth. Imagine it as in a school, a large group of students decides that they will burn fireworks on the campus just for fun. For example, let's say a happening occurred, then who would be responsible? Of course, the students are, but would they feel the depth of responsibility? No! Cause it happened because of a collective decision. That is what Plato did not trust: a decision made in a crowd, even if it is wrong, feels appealing, not because it is, it is because of the false confidence it gives.

When civic authority exists without competence, something strange happens. Decisions feel right because they are popular, even when they are poorly thought out. Responsibility becomes unclear. Since everyone took part, no one feels fully responsible for the result.

This makes reflection weaker. When a decision fails, blame is spread across the whole group. Instead of asking what went wrong, people defend the choice because it was collective. The system moves forward without learning from its mistakes.

Plato feared that democracy could create a culture where power feels ordinary. People become used to influencing without thinking about its weight. Civic authority becomes casual rather than careful. In such a society, mistakes no longer shock anyone. They become normal.

Voting without Understanding

Voting is often seen as the heart of democracy. It is the moment when taking part turns into real power. Through voting, people turn what they believe into decisions that affect everyone.

But voting shows preference, not understanding. A vote tells us what someone chose, not why they chose it. It does not show whether the decision came from careful thinking or a quick reaction because of popularity. It does not separate knowledge from emotion. Every vote counts the same, no matter how it was formed.

In a democracy, the vote of someone who understands an issue deeply counts the same as the vote of someone who does not understand it at all. Education and experience do not change the weight/value of the vote. Plato feared this equality, not because he thought some people were worth less, but because he believed decisions should reflect understanding and careful thinking, not just numbers.

This equality is intentional. Democracy values fairness in counting, not depth in reasoning. Everyone's choice is treated the same. But this design has consequences.

Plato believed that wisdom takes time. It grows through questioning and doubt. In *The Republic,* he argues that real learning often begins by realizing how little one knows. Voting hides this, making the process shorter, causing complex problems to be turned into simple choices. Just a vote eliminates the gap in the educated person's vote compared to the vote of an uneducated person.

This favors ideas that are easy to explain and easy to feel good about. *Simple stories spread faster than difficult truths. Ideas that require critical thinking are not valued by the crowd due to a lack of patience.* Over time, the system teaches people how to choose sides, but not how to think carefully.

Voting without understanding does not destroy democracy all at once. It weakens it slowly. Each decision builds habits of thought. When voting becomes routine without understanding and not critical thinking, it slowly eats democracy from a nation, where no one feels responsible if the future takes a darker turn.

Plato feared that people would begin to confuse voting with responsibility. Casting a vote would feel like doing one's duty, even when the issue itself was barely understood.

Knowledge vs Information

We often hear that modern democracy is stronger because people have more information. News is everywhere. Opinions, updates, explanations, and arguments are always available. It feels like a solution to an old problem. If everyone has access to information, then people can educate themselves.

But having information is not the same as knowing.

Information moves fast. It shows up, demands attention, and then disappears. It does not wait. Knowledge does. Knowledge takes time to form. It comes from thinking about something for long enough, critically to see its limits, its connections, and its uncertainty.

Democracy today often treats exposure as learning. If an issue is seen often, it is assumed to be understood. When something appears again and again, people begin to feel familiar with it. That feeling is mistaken for knowledge.

Plato warned about this long before modern media existed. He believed that opinion can easily pretend to be knowledge. When an idea is repeated often enough, it starts to feel solid, even if it has never been examined properly. Confidence grows not because something is true, but because it is familiar.

Democratic systems make this problem worse. They reward quick reactions. People who respond immediately appear involved and aware. Those who hesitate, who take time to think, are often ignored. This pushes citizens to form opinions before understanding has had time to develop.

Over time, democracy begins to function in this environment. Decisions are shaped by what is visible and recent, not by what has been studied carefully. People feel informed because they are surrounded by information, not because they have learned deeply.

Plato feared that this would quietly damage education itself. Learning would stop being something demanding. Knowing would mean recognizing a claim, not understanding it. The difference between someone who has studied an issue and someone who has only encountered it would slowly disappear.

In this situation, ignorance does not feel like ignorance. It feels like confidence. People speak clearly and comfortably about things they have never questioned seriously. Democracy rewards expression, not hesitation. Speaking matters more than thinking slowly.

Plato did not believe that access to information could replace education. Without discipline and patience, information does not lead to clarity. It increases confusion. Democracy assumes that more information creates better judgment. Plato doubted that assumption, and the doubt still matters.

Why Democracy Assumes Readiness

Democracy cannot easily question readiness without questioning itself. To ask whether citizens are prepared to rule is to risk undermining equality. If some are unprepared, who decides? On what grounds? The question threatens the foundation of participation.

And so democracy avoids it.

Readiness is treated as implicit. The act of inclusion becomes proof of capability. Education is encouraged but not required. Understanding is praised but not enforced. The system moves forward on trust.

Plato understood why this assumption exists. Democracy values dignity. It resists hierarchies of worth. To suggest that some should wait before participating feels like exclusion.

Yet avoidance carries a cost. When readiness is assumed rather than cultivated, education becomes secondary. Civic life proceeds faster than civic understanding. Power moves ahead of preparation.

This creates a permanent tension. Democracy depends on informed judgment, but it cannot guarantee it. It relies on citizens who think carefully, yet it does not structure itself to produce them.

Plato did not believe this tension could be eliminated easily. He believed it had to be faced honestly. A system that distributes power must also consider how that power is learned.

This chapter does not argue that democracy should impose tests or restrictions. It does not propose solutions. It identifies a structural gap: the distance between authority and preparation.

Democracy assumes readiness because it must. To pause would mean questioning equality itself. But assumption is not cultivation. Trust is not education.

Plato leaves us with an unresolved problem. If democracy depends on citizens who can think well, but does not require them to learn how, where does that responsibility lie? With the individual? With culture? With education itself?

This question does not accuse democracy of failure. It reveals a vulnerability. Power without preparation is not immediately destructive. It is quietly unstable.

And instability, Plato believed, rarely announces itself before it arrives.

6

Equality and the Illusion of Equal Judgment

India is the *largest democracy in the world.* Millions of people participate in decisions that shape the future of the country. Every adult citizen has one vote, regardless of education, awareness, access to information, or understanding of the issues involved. This fact is often presented as a strength of democracy. It shows equality. It shows inclusion. It shows trust in the people.

This equality feels just because it treats every citizen as politically equal. No one is officially told that their opinion matters less, nor are they excluded from participation. In a country as diverse as India, this equality carries moral importance. It protects dignity. It avoids hierarchy. It prevents power from being openly restricted to a small group.

But equality of voice does not mean equality of judgment.

Plato's discomfort

Plato's discomfort with democracy began here. He was not

disturbed by the idea that people should have dignity or that they should be protected from tyranny. What made him question was the assumption that judgment itself becomes reliable simply because it is shared by many people. He believed that governing a society was difficult, complex, and demanding, and that this complexity did not disappear when responsibility was spread across a crowd.

In a democracy like India, this problem becomes clearer because of scale. When millions of people participate, the differences in education, political understanding, and exposure become unavoidable. Some citizens follow issues closely. Some rely on fragments of information. Some vote based on emotion, identity, habit, or trust rather than understanding. Yet at the ballot box, all of this disappears. Every judgment is counted the same.

This equality is intentional. Democracy does not ask citizens to prove competence. It assumes that collective decision-making will correct individual mistakes. If one person lacks understanding, another person might compensate for it. Over time, the crowd is expected to reach good decisions. This belief feels reasonable, and it allows democracy to function without excluding people.

Plato did not trust this belief.

He did not think ignorance cancels itself out when multiplied. He believed it grows stronger. When many people share the same misunderstanding, it begins to feel correct. An agreement creates confidence, not truth (Chapter 5). In a large democracy, this confidence becomes even more powerful because numbers themselves feel convincing.

In India, collective decisions often carry immense weight. They shape laws, institutions, and long-term direction, and responsibility for these decisions is spread so widely that it becomes difficult to locate. When outcomes are good, the system is praised. When outcomes are harmful, the crowd blames each other. No single citizen feels fully responsible, because no single citizen feels decisive.

This is what Plato feared most. When power exists without clear responsibility, judgment becomes casual. Decisions feel lighter than they actually are. People participate, vote, support, and move on without fully confronting the consequences of those actions. Civic authority begins to feel ordinary rather than serious.

Equality of voice makes this possible. Because everyone participates, participation itself begins to feel sufficient. The act of voting feels like fulfilling one's duty, even when the issue itself is barely understood. Plato worried that people would begin to confuse participation with responsibility, and expression with thought.

In a country as large as India, this confusion does not come from bad intentions. It comes from structure. Democracy does not require citizens to understand complexity. It does not slow them down. It does not train judgment. It simply counts decisions. Over time, this trains habits of thinking where confidence matters more than reflection, and familiarity matters more than depth.

Plato believed judgment was a skill, not a natural right. He believed it required education, discipline, and the ability to doubt oneself. Democracy respects equality, but it does not cultivate these qualities by default. In fact, it often rewards the opposite. Those who speak clearly and confidently gain influence, even when understanding is shallow. Those who hesitate, question, or admit uncertainty are ignored.

This does not mean democracy is wrong. It means it is incomplete. Equality of voice protects citizens from exclusion, but it does not protect society from poor judgment. Plato's concern was never about denying people power. It was about what happens when power is exercised without preparation.

In the largest democracy in the world, this concern becomes impossible to ignore. Equality survives at scale. Understanding does not. The gap between the two grows wider, even as participation increases. Plato feared that in such a system, wisdom would slowly lose its place, not because people rejected it, but because the system stopped demanding it.

Equality feels fair. It feels moral. But Plato asked whether fairness in counting was enough. If judgment shapes the future of a nation, should it not also demand effort, responsibility, and thought? India's democracy forces this question into the open, not as an accusation, but as a reality.

The Comfort of Being Equal

Equality feels comforting because it removes tension from judgment.

When everyone is treated the same, no one has to face the uncomfortable question of whether they understand enough to make a decision.

In a democracy, being equal means that a person never has to explain how deeply they have thought about an issue or how much effort went into forming an opinion.

A person can speak, vote, and participate simply by existing as a citizen, without being asked to justify their level of understanding. This lack of pressure feels humane, especially in large and diverse societies where people come from very different backgrounds and experiences.

Plato understood why this sense of safety was attractive. He knew that most people do not like being reminded of their limits, and that questioning one's own understanding can feel unsettling.

Admitting that one does not know enough is difficult and often uncomfortable. Equality removes this discomfort by making all judgments appear equally valid, at least on the surface. When everyone's opinion is treated the same, no one feels exposed, and no one feels inferior.

But when judgment is treated as equal by default, the desire to improve it slowly weakens.

If every opinion carries the same weight, then thinking harder does not increase responsibility or influence. Over time, the effort required to understand complex issues begins to feel unnecessary. Participation alone starts to feel sufficient, and understanding becomes optional rather than important.

This was the quiet shift that Plato feared. He believed that good judgment required discomfort, doubt, and discipline, and that real thinking often begins when a person accepts that a problem is difficult and that understanding it will take time. Democracy, however, replaces this difficulty with reassurance. It tells citizens that their voice matters simply because it exists, not because it has been shaped carefully.

In a democracy like India, the largest democracy, this reassurance becomes especially powerful. People grow comfortable expressing strong opinions without examining them closely, because the system does not demand that they prove they are right, to think critically, but they just have a free voice. Confidence begins to feel earned through participation rather than understanding. Citizens are not asked to think or question themselves. Instead, the system rewards clarity and certainty, even when those qualities are not supported by deep thought.

Plato did not believe people were lazy or careless by nature. He believed that systems shape habits of thought. A system that prioritizes comfort slowly weakens the desire for seriousness. Equality, when separated from responsibility, trains people to feel secure in their judgment even when that judgment is shallow.

The danger here is not immediately apparent because comfort does not feel like a failure. It feels like fairness. It feels like respect. People believe they are acting responsibly simply by participating. However, Plato worried that a society too comfortable with its own thinking would cease to examine it. Equality would continue to protect participation, but it would also protect ignorance from being challenged.

In this sense, the comfort of being equal is not harmless. It quietly shapes how people relate to power. Judgment begins to feel ordinary instead of heavy. Decisions feel temporary and reversible rather than serious and lasting. Citizens grow used to influencing outcomes without sitting with the consequences of those choices.

Plato's discomfort was rooted here. He feared a society where equality removed the need for effort in critical thinking, and where comfort slowly took the place of wisdom without anyone caring and forgetting that their voices shape the nation but the ignorance of crowd makes it unnoticeable.

7

Can Democracy Teach Wisdom?

Democracy is often seen as a way that educates its citizens. It teaches people to speak, to vote, to protest, and to resist authority. Citizens in democratic polities learn early on that participation is an end in itself. Raising an opinion is considered a civic duty, and silence is frequently misinterpreted as cowardice. In this respect, democracy regulates not only power but also conduct, habits, and sentiment.

And yet, Plato would ask a question that democracy itself rarely asks.

Does it teach people how to think wisely, or does it only teach them how to make free choices?

This may at first sound like a simple question, but it is much deeper than we think. Wisdom seems abstract and personal; democracy seems practical and political. Yet Plato did not think the two could be separated. For Plato, political systems are also pedagogical systems: they educate their citizens, not by formal teaching, but through the rewards, the incentives, and the norms they encourage and consecrate. In due course, these incentives shape individual character and set society on its path.

In *The Republic,* Plato does not provide a straightforward response to this question. Instead, he approaches it by describing a specific kind of individual that democracy produces, which he calls the ***democratic man***. He is liberated, confident, and eloquent. He truly believes in equality, not merely between individuals but also among needs, opinions, and lifestyles. On the surface, he appears to be open-minded and tolerant. However, Plato argues that there is a serious problem lying below this apparent open-mindedness that the democratic man lives without hierarchy.

For Plato, wisdom requires inner order. Some desires must be guided, others restrained, and some rejected altogether. Reason must govern, not because desire is in and of itself evil, but rather because ungoverned desire yields instability. The *democratic man,* however, spurns this structural arrangement. He sustains the belief that no desire should rule over another. Each impulse is considered equal to any other. What he desires today is as valid as what he desired yesterday, even when the two desires conflict.

Plato presents this individual as being in constant flux: one day he is after knowledge, another day he is after pleasure, the third day it is ambition, then it is rest. None of these desires is felt or judged to be better or worse than any other; they are just different. He does not commit deeply to any single path - not because he is lazy but because such commitment seems a limitation. Choosing one value over another seems unfair. Disciplining a single desire seems oppressive.

This is where Plato's critique becomes serious.

Wisdom requires judgment according to Plato. It requires the capacity to discriminate that some choices are better than others, not on grounds of preference or popularity, but based on truth and long-term understanding. The democratic man struggles with this. When all choices become equal, judgment diminishes. Decision-making becomes reactionary. Life becomes a sequence of impulses rather than a coherent direction.

Here, Plato is not criticizing freedom. He does admit that the democratic man is freer than anyone else. He lives fearlessly of authority, with no rules that are too stringent. Yet, he questions whether this freedom amounts to anything. Freedom, severed from wisdom, has the risk of becoming meaningless. It gives license for movement with no direction, choice with no insight, and expression with no introspection.

This matters because democracy does not just tolerate the democratic man; it encourages him.

In democratic societies, the ability to voice an opinion is prized more highly than the ability to justify it rigorously. Confidence speaks more quickly than caution. And to change one's mind is seen as a sign of weakness rather than growth. It is little wonder that in such a world the democratic man feels at home. He can talk freely and never be obliged to think deeply. He can participate fully without ever being forced to confront his own limitations.

Plato believed that this kind of setting taught people to value choice as such over the quality of the choice.

Democratic citizens learn from a young age that having an opinion counts. Yet few are ever taught how opinions ought to be formed. The emphasis of education is on participation, not preparation. So individuals become comfortable expressing views without ever examining them. In this way, opinion can seem complete even when it is shallow. To speak comes to feel like thinking.

It is here that Plato would say democracy fails to nurture wisdom.

Wisdom is uncomfortable. It requires patience and self-discipline, and an admission of ignorance. It requires slowing down when the world around us promotes speed. And democratic life punishes slowness. Public deliberation rushes along. Decisions must be made now. Those who delay risk being left behind. In these circumstances, reflective thought becomes a liability.

Plato grasped that this was not the product of malice but of structural design. Democracy does not force wisdom on its practitioners. One can vote, argue, and influence outcomes without ever questioning one's own understanding. The system presumes a modicum of judgment that it is never concerned to instill.

Democracy requires that all citizens make decisions, influencing all. Laws, leaders, and values alike spring from the general judgment. Yet it cannot be trustworthy if uninstructed. Plato feared that democracy leans on wisdom, yet at the same time discourages the practices that would produce it.

This concern naturally led to another aspect of The Republic: the Allegory of the Cave. While it does not directly deal with democracy, it does reveal an important element in Plato's view of knowledge and belief. The prisoners in the cave are not cruel or stupid; they simply take for granted what they have always experienced. When one prisoner challenges the shadows and pursues the truth, he finds himself resisted, ridiculed, and shunned.

Plato's teaching is not, however, about ignorance but about comfort. People generally derive more security from familiar illusions than from difficult truths. Wisdom requires the disruption of this comfort, a process that is usually painful. Democracy, by contrast, tends to protect comfort. Ideas that painfully shake deeply held beliefs rarely gain much attention. Opinions that reassure gain easy access; those that unsettle are resisted.

This introduces another problem.

If wisdom requires challenging illusions, yet democracy rewards agreement, then wisdom will struggle to endure. The democratic man, formed in this environment, learns to avoid deep questioning. He is adept at expression but weak at reflection. He feels informed without being grounded.

Plato did not argue that democracy is doomed; he believed it to be incomplete.

It is not freedom alone that generates wisdom. It is not equality alone. It is not participation alone. Wisdom requires education of the soul, not just access to choice. This requires teaching people to deliberate on desires, to recognize ignorance, and to honor truth when it is unfashionable.

Without it, democracy risks being a system that amplifies voices without strengthening judgment.

This does not mean that Plato was arguing for the silencing of people. He did not argue that opinion ought to disappear. The concern was balance: opinion has to be tempered with understanding. Liberty needs to be coupled with discipline. Choice needs to be coupled with responsibility.

The democratic man embodies what transpires when this balance is lost.

He is not cruel. He is not malicious. He is not ignorant by nature. He is simply untrained. And a society filled with untrained decision makers, no matter how free, becomes unstable. Decisions swing by mood. Values drift with fads. Wisdom becomes optional.

Thus, if we ask whether democracy can teach wisdom, Plato's reply is sobering and unsettling. Democracy may make space for wisdom, but it does not ensure it. It might allow for the presence of wise voices, but does not demand their propagation.

It can protect the freedom to think, but it does not demand reflective deliberation.

Whether democracy teaches wisdom depends not so much on its structure as on whether it demands intellectual responsibility from those who participate within it. Without that demand, freedom becomes noise, and choice becomes habit. Plato leaves us with a challenge, not with a conclusion. If democracy distributes power broadly, then all participants must learn to exercise power with wisdom.

> *If it cannot impart this capacity, then wisdom must emerge from somewhere else, or it will surely disappear beneath confidence, comfort, and constant opinion.*

8

The Vote of Popularity

In early *Athens*, the birthplace of democracy, even military generals were elected by the general people, even on matters as serious as war. At first, this may sound admirable, a system where the state trusted its citizens enough to give everyone the right to vote. Power was not locked away with kings or inherited by birth. Ordinary people had a voice, and that voice mattered.

For many, this felt like the highest form of freedom. Decisions that affected the entire city were not imposed from above but emerged from collective choice. *Athens* believed that when people ruled themselves, tyranny could never take hold. Democracy promised fairness through participation and equality through shared authority.

Plato never had a problem with this right of the people themselves. He did not believe that citizens should be silenced or excluded. What troubled him was a deeper question that most people never stopped to ask. Were the people voting for generals because of their skill and strategic thinking, or simply because they liked their confidence, appearance, or the way they spoke?

This question may sound small, but for Plato, it revealed something fundamental about democracy. Choosing a military general was not a symbolic decision. It was not just about representation or fairness. It was about life and death. A wrong choice could lead to defeat, suffering, and destruction. Yet the process of choosing did not demand knowledge. It demanded popularity.

To Plato, this revealed a serious problem. Democracy treated all judgment as equal, even when the subject demanded expertise. A vote did not measure understanding. It measured preference. What felt right to the crowd often mattered more than what actually was right.

Plato believed that some tasks required training. No one would trust a sick person's life to a random vote. No one would choose a doctor based on charm alone. In daily life, people naturally understand that skill matters. But when it came to politics, this understanding seemed to disappear. Democracy assumed that collective choice would somehow correct individual ignorance.

Plato did not trust this assumption.

He believed ignorance does not cancel itself out when multiplied. Instead, it gains confidence. When many people share the same misunderstanding, it begins to feel true. Agreement creates comfort, not accuracy. The crowd becomes sure of itself, even when it is wrong.

To make this clearer, imagine a similar situation in a classroom. The students are electing a class monitor. Two students stand for the election. One is thoughtful and can actually think, plan, and work for the benefit of the class. He understands responsibility, listens to others, and takes problems seriously. The other is confident, funny, and speaks well in front of everyone. He makes the class laugh and promises easy solutions.

In most cases, the second student is likely to be elected. Not because he is more capable, but because he is more likable. The vote reflects emotion, not judgment. The students are not evil or careless. They are simply human. They choose what feels good in the moment.

Plato saw *Athens* in the same way. Important decisions were being made not based on knowledge, but on popularity. Leadership slowly became a reward for persuasion rather than responsibility.

In *Athens,* speaking well mattered deeply. Public life depended on speeches. Leaders addressed large assemblies, juries, and councils. The ability to persuade was a power. Plato noticed that those who spoke clearly and confidently gained influence, even if they lacked real understanding. Meanwhile, those who hesitated, questioned themselves, or spoke cautiously were ignored.

This worried Plato because real thinking is often slow. It involves doubt, revision, and uncertainty. A person who truly understands a complex issue rarely speaks with complete confidence. They see complications. They recognize limits. In contrast, someone who understands very little often speaks with great certainty. They see no difficulty because they see no depth.

Democracy, Plato believed, rewarded the second type of person.

This does not mean Plato hated freedom. In fact, he understood its appeal deeply. He knew why people wanted equality and participation. Freedom feels safe. It feels just. It feels human. Plato did not want to return to tyranny or absolute rule. His fear was different. He feared that freedom without discipline would slowly destroy wisdom.

The example of generals was only one part of a larger pattern. *Athens* trusted the crowd in courts as well. Large juries made decisions about guilt and punishment. Ordinary citizens judged complex legal and moral cases. Again, Plato asked the same question. Were these decisions guided by careful reasoning or by emotion and persuasion?

Plato watched his own teacher, Socrates, stand before such a jury. Socrates did not flatter the crowd. He did not promise comfort. He questioned assumptions and challenged beliefs. The jury responded with anger and fear. They voted to execute him.

For Plato, this was not an accident. It was a warning.

The crowd did not kill Socrates because it hated the truth. It killed him because the truth was uncomfortable. Democracy protected the right to speak, but it did not protect wisdom from rejection. The same system that allowed free thought also allowed the silencing of it.

This created a deep conflict in Plato's thinking.

He wanted a society guided by reason. But he saw that reason does not naturally rise to the top in a democracy. Emotion moves faster. Confidence spreads more easily. Popular ideas dominate careful ones. Plato struggled with this reality.

Should leadership belong to those chosen by the many, or to those trained to understand what they are doing? If wisdom is rare, how can a system that treats all judgment equally protect it? And if power is given to the untrained, who is responsible when things go wrong?

Plato never answered these questions easily. His writing shows hesitation. He criticizes democracy sharply, but he does not fully abandon it. He imagines philosopher-kings, but he knows they may never exist. He believes education is the solution, yet he knows education itself takes time and authority.

This is where Plato's confusion becomes clear.

He believed that democracy assumed readiness. It gave people power first and hoped understanding would follow. Plato thought this was dangerous. Power shapes outcomes immediately. Education shapes people slowly. When power moves faster than wisdom, mistakes become permanent.

In the classroom example, the class monitor's poor decisions may cause small problems. But in a state, poor leadership causes real harm. Wars are lost. Laws fail. People suffer. Yet democracy treats these decisions as ordinary choices, similar to everyday preferences.

Plato feared that this would train people to think lightly about serious matters. Voting would feel routine. Responsibility would feel shared. No single person would feel accountable. When everyone decides, no one feels fully responsible.

This is why Plato worried about the crowd.

A crowd feels strong, but it also feels safe from blame. Individual judgment dissolves into collective approval. People defend decisions not because they are right, but because they were popular. Over time, reflection weakens. Admitting error feels like admitting weakness.

Plato believed this habit was dangerous.

Even in the modern world, this pattern still exists. Confident and loud speakers often receive support, while experts who understand long-term consequences but are not good at public speaking remain unheard. Public debate rewards certainty more than accuracy. Changing one's mind is seen as failure, not growth.

Plato's concern was not limited to his own time. It was a warning about how democracy can mistake confidence for competence.

He did not argue that people should be silenced. He argued that judgment must be trained. Wisdom does not appear automatically when people are given freedom. It must be cultivated. Without education, freedom becomes directionless. Choice becomes habit. Opinion becomes authority.

Plato's fear was quiet, not dramatic. He did not predict immediate collapse. He predicted a gradual decline. A society that rewards popularity over understanding slowly loses its ability to think deeply. Decisions become reactive. Values drift. Wisdom becomes optional.

The example of *Athens* choosing generals shows this clearly. Democracy trusted the crowd to decide everything, even when expertise mattered most. Plato watched this trust turn into carelessness. Not because people were bad, but because the system asked too little of them.

This is what Plato was truly thinking.

He was not against democracy as an idea. He was against untrained power. He believed that a society that gives power to everyone must also teach everyone how to use it wisely. Without that balance, democracy risks becoming a system where noise replaces thought, and popularity replaces responsibility.

Plato leaves us with a realization. The danger is not that people choose wrongly once. The danger is that they choose out on looks, not by thinking deeply about it. On a small scale, it is fine, but in a democracy, it can tear it apart.

9

Democracy to Dictatorship

Adolf Hitler, a great, confident, passionate speaker, but also a *great killer of both people and democracy.* He is the perfect example of how democracy can be destroyed in the way Plato feared, how democracy itself, when it turns into a vote of popularity without education, can slowly create a dictator, and how a crowd can end up giving power to the very man who later takes that power away from them.

Plato did not fear democracy because he hated freedom or equality; he feared it because he understood something uncomfortable about human nature. He understood that people do not always choose what is right; they often choose what feels right, and when feeling becomes more important than thinking, democracy becomes fragile without anyone realizing it. The danger does not arrive with violence at first; it arrives with applause, with speeches, with confidence, with the feeling that finally someone understands the people.

Hitler did not rise as a dictator in one moment; he rose slowly, step by step, through a system that was still called democratic, and that is exactly why his rise matters so much when trying to understand Plato. Plato feared that democracy could destroy itself from the inside, not because people are evil, but because people are emotional, tired, scared, and easily influenced when life becomes difficult, and Germany at that time was a perfect example of a society under pressure.

Germany after the First World War was not just economically broken; it was mentally broken. People felt humiliated, angry, and uncertain about their future, and when a nation loses pride and stability at the same time, it begins to search desperately for meaning, strength, and direction. Jobs were disappearing, money was losing value, families were struggling to survive, and political debates felt endless and useless to people who wanted immediate relief, not careful explanations.

Plato would have understood this situation deeply because he believed that when people are suffering, they do not have the patience for complex truth; they want simple answers, and simple answers are usually the most dangerous ones. A society in pain does not ask who is most knowledgeable; it asks who sounds most confident, and confidence can exist without wisdom. Sometimes it exists best without it.

This is where Hitler became powerful, not because he was wise, but because he was certain, because he spoke as if there were no doubts, no complications, no long paths, only enemies to defeat and greatness to restore. He did not ask people to think deeply; he asked them to believe strongly, and belief is easier than thought when life feels heavy.

Plato feared that democracy would turn politics into a competition of persuasion rather than a search for truth, and Hitler mastered persuasion. He knew how to speak to emotions, how to turn anger into unity, how to make fear feel like strength, and once a crowd starts feeling united behind one voice, disagreement becomes uncomfortable, and criticism begins to feel like betrayal.

Democracy depends on disagreement, but crowds often hate disagreement when they are afraid. Plato saw this long before Hitler existed. He watched how crowds in Athens reacted emotionally, how they could be convinced quickly, how they could silence uncomfortable voices, and he realized that democracy gives power to the people but does not automatically teach the people how to use that power wisely.

When people vote, the vote does not measure understanding; it does not measure knowledge of economics, war, law, or long-term consequences. It measures preference, and preference is shaped by emotion, fear, hope, and identity. This is not always wrong, but it becomes dangerous when emotion replaces judgment completely, when confidence becomes more important than competence.

Hitler benefited from exactly this weakness. He presented himself as the answer to chaos, the voice of order in a noisy political world, and people supported him not because they studied deeply what would happen, but because they felt relief listening to him. Plato feared this moment more than any other, the moment when freedom starts to feel like a burden and control starts to feel like comfort.

Democracy did not collapse in Germany overnight. It weakened slowly. Laws changed gradually. Rights were restricted step by step. Each decision was justified as necessary, each restriction was explained as temporary, and that is one of the most dangerous illusions Plato warned about, because when freedom is taken away slowly, people adjust to the loss instead of resisting it.

At first, Hitler was not seen by many as a tyrant; he was seen as a solution, and that is the most frightening form of power, when a dictator does not look like a dictator yet. Plato believed that tyranny does not always announce itself openly; sometimes it arrives quietly, supported by the people who believe they are protecting themselves.

Another part of Plato's fear was manipulation. He believed that once leaders understand how to control emotion, they can control judgment. Hitler understood how to give people enemies to blame, how to create simple stories where suffering had clear causes and clear targets, and when people believe their pain comes from an enemy, they stop questioning the leader who promises to defeat that enemy.

This is how democracy begins to rot internally. People stop asking whether the leader is right and start asking whether the leader is on their side. Truth becomes less important than loyalty. Reason becomes less important than unity. Plato feared this shift deeply because once loyalty replaces reason, freedom is already dying.

Education was Plato's answer to this problem. Not education as memorizing facts, but education as training judgment, training the mind to slow down, to question itself, to detect manipulation, and to resist emotional shortcuts. Without this kind of education, democracy becomes easy to manipulate, because people react instead of thinking.

Hitler's rise shows what happens when political education is weak. People did not question enough. They trusted too quickly. They followed confidence instead of competence. And once power was concentrated, it did not stop at Germany's borders. Dictatorship rarely stays contained, because domination becomes its logic.

This is where the destruction of democracy turned into the destruction of Germany itself. Once Hitler had control, the state became a tool for expansion, violence, and ideology. The same emotional energy that brought him to power was redirected outward, and the result was war, suffering, and devastation on a massive scale.

World War II was not just a war started by one man; it was the outcome of a system that failed to protect itself from manipulation. A democracy that lost its judgment created a dictatorship, and that dictatorship led the nation into destruction. Cities were destroyed. Millions died. Germany itself was left broken and occupied by the end of the war.

Plato would not have been surprised by this ending. He believed that leadership without wisdom eventually harms both others and itself. A society that rewards persuasion over understanding does not become strong; it becomes reckless. And recklessness always returns home.

This is why Hitler is not just a historical figure in this chapter; he is a mirror that reflects Plato's fear in reality. Plato did not predict Hitler, but he predicted the pattern that made Hitler possible. A society in pain. Weak education. Emotional politics. A confident manipulator. A crowd that chooses relief over responsibility. A democracy that slowly hands over its freedom.

The most disturbing part is not that people supported Hitler, but that many believed they were doing the right thing at the time. Plato feared this exact blindness because when people stop questioning themselves, they become dangerous not only to others but to themselves.

Democracy is not destroyed only by enemies from outside. Sometimes it is destroyed by the choices made inside it. Sometimes it collapses not with resistance, but with agreement.

Plato's warning was never meant to attack democracy; it was meant to protect it. He believed freedom must be guided by wisdom; otherwise, freedom becomes unstable. Voting must be supported by judgment; otherwise, voting becomes a weapon against itself.

Hitler shows what happens when democracy forgets this balance. He shows how popularity without education can turn freedom into control, how confidence without wisdom can turn hope into destruction, and how a system built to protect people can end up harming them.

This chapter is not written to compare times or accuse societies. It is written to show a pattern. A pattern Plato saw long before modern history existed. A pattern that repeats when emotion replaces thought and popularity replaces responsibility.

> *If democracy once created Hitler, then Plato's question becomes impossible to ignore. When people choose their leaders, are they choosing what is right or what feels right?*

Plato's Fear Became Real

Once democracy begins to weaken in this way, the most brutal change is not the loss of laws or institutions, but the change inside people themselves. Plato feared that long before people lose freedom officially, they lose the habit of using it. They stop questioning, not because questioning is banned at first, but because questioning feels time-consuming, risky, and unnecessary when someone else is already deciding for them.

At this stage, people do not feel oppressed. In fact, many feel relieved. Decisions feel simpler. Responsibility feels lighter. Life feels more predictable. Plato understood this temptation very well. Freedom demands effort. It demands thinking, disagreement, uncertainty, and patience. Control, on the other hand, demands obedience, and obedience feels easy when life is already difficult.

This is the moment where democracy does not need to be destroyed by force. It dissolves quietly. People begin to accept limits on freedom not because they hate freedom, but because they are afraid of chaos returning. They tell themselves that a little less freedom is a small price to pay for stability, and Plato believed that once people accept this trade, they rarely notice how much they are giving away.

Another thing Plato feared deeply was silence. Not silence imposed immediately, but silence chosen voluntarily. When people see others punished, attacked, or isolated for speaking differently, they learn quickly. They tell themselves it is safer not to speak. They convince themselves that staying quiet is wisdom. Slowly, silence spreads, and when silence becomes normal, resistance becomes strange.

Plato believed that a society does not lose its freedom all at once. It loses it through habits. The habit of not questioning. The habit of agreeing without thinking. The habit of ignorance.

And once these habits form, even obvious injustice begins to feel ordinary.

This is also why Plato believed thinkers become dangerous in such systems. People who question, who doubt, who think deeply remind others of the freedom they have abandoned. Instead of being admired, these thinkers are mocked, ignored, or treated as enemies. Education itself begins to look suspicious, because education teaches people to pause, and a system built on obedience cannot afford too much pausing.

Over time, people start to change their own beliefs to survive. Instead of saying something is wrong, they say it is necessary. Instead of saying something is unjust, they say it is temporary. Plato feared this inner adjustment more than open violence, because once people convince themselves that control is justified, tyranny no longer needs to force obedience. It receives it willingly.

This is how democracy finishes its transformation. Not with resistance, but with acceptance. Not with outrage, but with explanation. People begin defending the system that controls them because admitting the truth would mean admitting their own role in creating it.

Plato believed this was the final tragedy. Not that people are oppressed, but that they forget they ever had a choice.

And this is where Plato's warning becomes complete. He was not writing about one city or one time. He was writing about a pattern that appears whenever popularity replaces wisdom and emotion replaces judgment. He feared that democracy, without education and responsibility, could slowly train people to surrender the very freedom it was meant to protect.

This chapter is not meant to argue that democracy always

fails. It is meant to show that democracy is fragile. It survives only when people are willing to think, question, and take responsibility for their choices. Without that effort, democracy becomes vulnerable to confident voices that promise comfort instead of truth.

Plato's fear was never about people having power. It was about people being unprepared for power.

When citizens stop asking difficult questions, when they stop valuing knowledge, when they stop resisting emotional shortcuts, democracy begins to change its shape. It still looks like democracy from the outside, but inside, something essential has already been lost.

This is why the road from democracy to dictatorship is rarely dramatic. It is quiet. It is gradual. It is built from choices that feel reasonable in the moment.

And by the time people realize what has happened, they no longer recognize the system they helped create.

Plato did not offer an easy solution to this problem. He offered a warning. A warning that freedom without wisdom is unstable, and that a society that chooses comfort over responsibility risks losing both.

> *The question Plato leaves us with is not about history, and it is not about leaders. It is about ourselves. When we choose, are we choosing carefully, or are we choosing comfortably? Because that answer decides whether democracy remains a space for freedom, or slowly becomes the place where freedom disappears.*

10

For Democracy

Democracy is often treated as something that exists by itself, something stable, automatic, and unquestionable, as if the moment it is achieved it becomes permanent and no longer needs attention, but when one looks more carefully at how easily democracy can be weakened, redirected, and slowly reshaped, it becomes clear that democracy does not survive simply because it exists, it survives only under certain conditions, and understanding those conditions matters far more than praising the idea without reflection.

Much of the criticism aimed at democracy is dismissed because of the belief that to question democracy is to stand against it, but this belief misses a deeper truth, because systems that cannot be questioned are not strong, they are fragile ones, and Plato's concern was never about tearing democracy apart, but about revealing the points where it quietly depends on human judgment while doing very little to prepare humans to judge well.

What Plato feared was not the act of choosing itself, but the act of choosing without responsibility. He saw democracy as a system that spreads power widely among citizens, but does not automatically develop the standards or discipline required to use that power carefully, and when power expands faster than wisdom, the system begins to rely less on understanding and more on chance, persuasion, emotion, and impulse.

This concern did not emerge from theory alone. For Plato, *Athens* was not an abstract political idea or a distant example; it was his home, a living city filled with debates, speeches, assemblies, votes, pride, ambition, and rivalry. It was a place where citizens gathered to decide matters of war and peace, law and punishment, leadership and exile, often in open spaces where emotion traveled faster than reflection and confident voices carried more influence than experience.

Athens believed deeply in participation. Citizens were expected to speak, to vote, to judge, and to rule. On the surface, this appeared to be the highest form of freedom, because no single voice ruled continuously and no individual stood permanently above the law. Yet Plato noticed a contradiction at the heart of this system, because while every citizen had the right to speak, not every citizen had the discipline to think deeply, and while every citizen had the right to vote, not every citizen understood what their decision truly meant.

He observed that decisions were often shaped not by careful understanding but by temporary passion. A powerful speech could sway an assembly. A loud voice could silence hesitation. Public opinion could shift rapidly, not because truth had changed, but because emotions had. In these moments, democracy appeared energetic and alive, yet Plato wondered whether this energy reflected purposeful direction or simply movement without control.

Here, Plato's thinking becomes careful rather than dismissive. He did not argue that people should not govern themselves. Instead, he questioned whether self-governance without preparation could remain stable over time. Democracy, in his view, assumes a certain level of wisdom among citizens, but it does not guarantee that this wisdom exists, and when that assumption fails, democracy does not collapse suddenly; it drifts.

This idea of drifting is important. Plato believed that political decline rarely feels like decline while it is happening. Life continues. Decisions are still made. Votes are still counted. Assemblies still gather. Yet slowly, the quality of judgment shifts, almost unnoticed, until outcomes begin to lose contact with reason altogether.

To express this pattern, Plato preferred analogy over instruction, because analogy allows understanding without force. Among his many analogies, the image of the ship remains one of the clearest ways to understand what democracy requires.

> *Imagine a ship at sea. The ship belongs to everyone on board because the direction it takes determines whether all survive. Now imagine that the crew must decide who should steer. Some argue that everyone should have an equal say because everyone is affected by the outcome. Others argue that steering requires knowledge of navigation, winds, currents, and stars.*
>
> *Plato did not deny the equality of those on the ship.*

> *What he rejected was the assumption that equality of presence automatically means equality of judgment. The ship does not respond to intentions. The sea does not adjust itself according to popularity. The stars do not move because someone speaks confidently. Navigation demands understanding whether or not that understanding is admired.*

In Plato's view, democracy often treats the ship as if it will move correctly simply because the decision was made collectively. But the sea does not recognize votes. It responds only to direction, and direction requires knowledge.

At the same time, Plato did not argue for absolute command by one ruler. He feared tyranny as much as he feared disorder. What he sought was balance, a system in which those who decide understand the weight of decision, and in which citizens recognize that choosing a direction is not the same as choosing a preference.

Of all the cities of his time, *Athens* troubled him most in this regard. The city cherished freedom, but freedom without discipline turned into excess. Too many voices spoke at once, and not all of them were thoughtful. The crowd became skilled at reacting, but less skilled at reflecting. Plato noticed that reason often arrived too late, after decisions had already been made.

He also observed something more subtle. When mistakes occurred, responsibility disappeared. No single person felt accountable. The decision belonged to everyone, and therefore to no one. This diffusion of responsibility made it easier to repeat errors, because regret had no clear place to settle.

Plato believed that democracy needed more than laws to survive. It needed character. It needed citizens trained not only to speak, but to listen, not only to vote, but to pause, not only to feel, but to question feeling itself.

For Plato, education was not about separating rulers from ordinary people. It was about strengthening citizens so they could rule themselves without destroying what they ruled. Without this preparation, he feared democracy would reward surface qualities such as confidence, charm, and certainty, while quietly sidelining patience, doubt, and long thinking.

Athens gave Plato many reasons for this concern. Leaders rose and fell quickly. Policies changed direction. Decisions made in excitement were later regretted. Plato did not see these as rare failures, but as signs of a system that trusted judgment without training it.

Yet even in criticism, Plato did not abandon democracy. He continued to question it because he believed questioning was its only protection. A democracy that refuses to examine itself becomes a performance rather than a process, celebrating participation while neglecting understanding.

The ship returns here, not as a warning, but as a responsibility. If the ship belongs to everyone, then everyone shares the duty to ensure it is steered well. Voting is not only about choosing who holds the wheel, but about taking responsibility for the journey itself.

Plato feared that when citizens stop caring about direction and focus only on expression, democracy becomes noise rather than order. Voices multiply, meaning things. Freedom remains, but purpose weakens. The ship continues to move, but its destination becomes uncertain.

This does not mean democracy must fail. Plato never claimed that. He believed democracy survives when citizens understand that freedom requires effort, attention, restraint, and the courage to resist easy answers and attractive rhetoric.

Athens showed Plato both the beauty and danger of collective power, how human energy can create a culture of debate and imagination, and how the same energy, when left without reflection, can become impulsive and destructive. Democracy, for Plato, was never a finished solution, but a tension, something unfinished, requiring constant correction, continuous education, and awareness of its own weaknesses.

The ship remains unresolved for a reason. Plato did not appoint an eternal leader for the ship. He questioned whether those choosing the direction understood what steering truly meant. He asked whether freedom was being treated as responsibility or simply as entitlement.

Athens did not answer him clearly. History has not answered him either. Democracy remains open, incomplete, dependent not only on ideals, but on the people who inhabit it.

> *Plato left the question where it belongs, not in systems or laws, but in human judgment itself. Democracy does not fail because people participate. It fails when participation stops being serious, stop thinking, stop understanding, and starts ignoring; That's where democracy fails. A system which require constant questioning and is not questioned*

that's where it start to tear apart.

11

Plato's Unfinished Question

Throughout this book, Plato has appeared not as an enemy of democracy, but as its most uncomfortable critic. He did not reject freedom, equality, or participation. What troubled him was something deeper: the assumption that these values naturally produce wisdom. For him, the problem of democracy was never simply political. It was intellectual.

Plato believed that every system of rule encourages a certain kind of thinking. Some systems demand discipline and restraint. Others reward obedience. Democracy, he feared, encourages confidence without understanding. It invites participation without preparation. It gives power to opinion while asking little about how that opinion was formed.

Because of this, Plato was never a comfortable figure in public life. To many citizens of Athens, his ideas felt arrogant or detached. He questioned popular beliefs, challenged respected leaders, and refused to flatter public opinion. From the perspective of the crowd, Plato did not sound democratic. He sounded distant, even threatening. His insistence on expertise and education appeared to undermine equality.

To governments, Plato was equally unsettling. He did not offer praise. He did not promise stability. He did not provide simple control rules. Instead, he questioned legitimacy itself. He asked whether rulers understood justice, whether laws were guided by wisdom, and whether power without knowledge could ever be safe. These questions made him inconvenient rather than useful.

Plato understood that philosophers are rarely welcomed by either the crowd or authority. To the public, they appear critical and elitist. To rulers, they appear disruptive and impractical. Yet Plato believed this discomfort was necessary. A society that feels comfortable with its own thinking, he believed, has already stopped thinking.

Across the chapters before this one, a pattern has emerged. Opinion rises faster than knowledge. Crowds think differently from individuals. Persuasion often defeats understanding. Voices multiply, yet attention concentrates. None of these outcomes requires bad intentions. They arise naturally from the structure itself.

Plato's concern was not that people are incapable of wisdom. It was that wisdom requires conditions that democracy does not automatically provide. Knowledge demands time, education, humility, and a willingness to admit ignorance. Democratic life, by contrast, rewards immediacy, certainty, and visibility. The two are not enemies, but they are not aligned.

This leaves democracy in a difficult position. It values freedom of expression, yet struggles to protect the depth of thought. It promises equality, yet produces unequal influence. It invites everyone to speak, yet rarely teaches how to think. Plato did not believe these tensions could be solved easily. He believed they had to be acknowledged honestly.

What makes Plato enduring is not that he offered solutions governments could apply, but that he refused to let societies rest comfortably in their assumptions. His philosophy acts less like a blueprint and more like a mirror. It reflects the weaknesses that power prefers not to see.

Plato never offered a final answer that satisfies modern readers. His ideal state feels distant, even unrealistic. But perhaps that was never the point. Plato was less interested in designing a perfect system than in exposing a dangerous belief: that truth naturally emerges from popularity, and wisdom from numbers.

This book does not argue that democracy should be abandoned. It also does not argue that Plato was right. It argues that Plato was serious. He took thinking seriously, education seriously, and responsibility seriously. He believed that the health of a society depends not only on who rules, but on how its people think, and gives you another lens to see ***democracy***.

Plato's unfinished question remains with us. If democracy gives power to the people, what kind of people must they become for that power to be used wisely? And if a society cannot answer that question, can any system of rule truly save it?

www.ingramcontent.com/pod-product-compliance
Ingram Content Group UK Ltd.
Pitfield, Milton Keynes, MK11 3LW, UK
UKHW041311190726
13845UKWH00025B/202